ATOS Book Level: _____ 2.3 _____
AR Points: _____ 0.5 _____
Quiz #: _10191_ [✓] RP [ ] LS [ ] VP
Lexile: _____

MY FIRST LOOK

AT COUNTRIES

IRAN IS A BEAUTIFUL COUNTRY

Iran

ADELE RICHARDSON

CREATIVE EDUCATION

AN OLD COUNTRY

Iran is a very old country. It is one of the oldest countries in the world! People have lived there for more than 8,000 years. The first people to live in Iran were farmers.

Iran is on the **continent** of Asia. It is in the southwest part of the continent. Southwest is the bottom left part of Asia on a map. The area is also called the "Middle East."

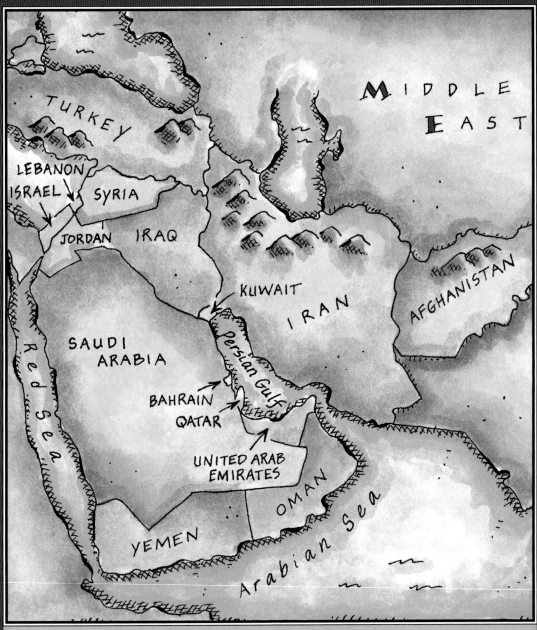

A MAP OF THE MIDDLE EAST

Iran is a big country. It is a little bigger than the state of Alaska. Iran is shaped like a triangle. Seven other countries touch Iran. Water touches the top and bottom of Iran.

DRY LAND AND MOUNTAINS

Iran does not get much rain. A lot of the country is **desert**. It is hot in the desert. Not many plants or trees grow there. Iran does not have many rivers. All of the lakes in Iran are salty.

Iran has lots of small earthquakes every year. Big earthquakes happen about every 10 years.

The middle of Iran is a big **plateau** (*plah-TOW*). It covers about half of the country. Grass grows in some places on the plateau. It is called camel grass.

There are many mountains in Iran. Some of the mountains are very high. They have snow on them all year. Some people climb Iran's mountains for fun!

A person can stand

almost anywhere in Iran

and see a mountain.

ANIMALS IN IRAN

Lots of animals live in Iran. Some are small, such as rabbits and gerbils. Others are big, such as bears. Turtles, snakes, and frogs live in Iran, too.

Many birds live in Iran. Storks and owls live there. Golden eagles fly high in the sky. Iran has lots of flamingoes. They eat shrimps. The shrimps make them look pink!

A PINK-COLORED FLAMINGO DRINKING WATER

The Asian black bear lives in Iran. It is **endangered**. It has mostly black fur. The fur on its chest is white. The bear has long neck fur. It looks like a lion's mane!

ASIAN BLACK BEARS ARE ALSO CALLED MOON BEARS

The People

Most of Iran's people live in cities. Most of the cities are in the west, or left, part of Iran. Iran's biggest city is called Tehran (*Teh-RAN*). It is the **capital**. More than 10 million people live in Tehran.

Some people in Iran live in small towns. Some of their homes are made of wood. Others are made of bricks of mud.

People in Iran drink hot tea.
They place sugar cubes in
their mouth while drinking it!

WOMEN IN IRAN COVER THEIR HEADS IN PUBLIC

People in Iran like to spend time with their families and friends. They like to eat with each other. Many people like to hike. Some people like to go on picnics. No matter what they are doing, people in Iran like to have fun!

THIS OLD BUILDING HAS PICTURES CARVED IN IT

Hands-on: Right to Left

People in Iran write from right to left. Have you ever tried to write that way?

What You Need

A piece of paper
A pencil

What You Do

1. Start at the paper's right side. Write the first letter of your name.
2. Now write the rest of your name to the left. If your name is Kim, it would look like this: miK.
3. Look around for other things you can spell. Do you see a dog or cat? Can you see a lamp? It is not easy to write this way. But it is fun to try!

A BOY WRITING IN IRAN'S LANGUAGE

Index

Words to Know

capital—the main city in a country

continent—one of Earth's seven big pieces of land

desert—a dry, sandy area where few plants and trees grow

endangered—an animal that might die out so that there are no more left on Earth

plateau—an area of high, flat land

Read More

Bauer, Brandy. *Iran: A Question and Answer Book*. Mankato, Minn.: Fact Finders, 2005.

Doak, Robin S. *Iran*. Minneapolis: Compass Point Books, 2004.

Kaplan, Leslie C. *A Primary Source Guide to Iran*. New York: PowerKids Press, 2005.

Explore the Web

Country at a Glance: Iran http://www.cyberschoolbus.org/infonation/index.asp?id=364

Enchanted Learning Outline Map http://www.enchantedlearning.com/asia/iran/outlinemap/index.shtml

World Flag Database: Flags of Iran http://www.flags.net/country.php?country=IRAN&section=CURR